ENGLISH

Author

Kath Jordan

CONTENTS

READING FICTION

READING POETRY

READING NON-FICTION

READING MEDIA TEXTS

WRITING

SHAKESPEARE

SPELLING, PUNCTUATION AND GRAMMAR

WHAT TO EXPECT IN YOUR EXAMS

At the end of Year 9 you will receive two National Curriculum levels. The first is from your key stage 3 SATS (Standard Assessment Tests), the second is your Teacher Assessment level given by your class teacher. This book is designed to help you achieve the best level you can.

ATTAINMENT TARGETS

The National Curriculum for English is split into three Attainment Targets.

- AT1 Speaking and Listening: this is not tested in your SATS but it does count towards your Teacher Assessment level.
- AT2 Reading: Both SATS papers test your understanding and response to a variety of written texts.
- AT3 Writing: Both SATS papers test your written expression and accuracy.

NATIONAL CURRICULUM LEVELS

Each Attainment Target is split into eight levels. The expected level for 14-year-olds is level 5. Your SATS result will be an overall level for AT2 and AT3. Your Teacher Assessment level will be an overall level for AT1, AT2 and AT3. Each section of this book explains what you need to do to reach level 5 and above.

Exam Advice Check-list

- Look closely at the amount of time and the number of marks available for each question.
- Make sure you allow yourself time to check your answers carefully.
- Make sure you read the questions carefully and answer them fully.
- Follow the instructions, e.g. there are three questions in section C but you only have to answer one.
- Plan your answers, especially in Paper 1C and Paper 2.
- Bring a watch into the exam or make sure you can see a clock.

PAPER ONE

SECTION: A

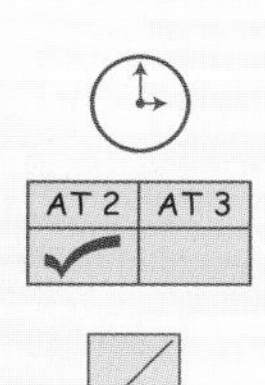

Time: 30 Minutes	Fiction or non-fiction
Tests understanding and response	2 questions
Marks = 17	

SECTION: B

Time: 20 minutes	Often poetry or media but could also be fiction or non-fiction
Tests understanding and response	1 question
Marks = 11	

SECTION: C

Time: 35 minutes + 5 minutes checking	Writing imaginative/ descriptive or persuasive or informative
Tests written expression	1 question from choice of 3
Marks = 33	

Total time: 1 hour 30 minutes + 15 minutes reading time	Materials: one question paper and one answer booklet

PAPER TWO

SHAKESPEARE

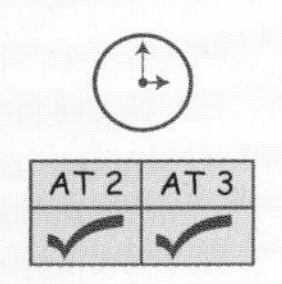

Time: 1 hour 15 minutes

Tests understanding and response and written expression.

Macbeth One question on each set scene. Choose one.

or

Twelfth Night One question on each set scene. Choose one.

or

Henry V One question on each set scene. Choose one.

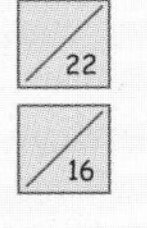

Marks = 22 understanding and response   16 written expression

Materials: one question paper, one booklet containing set scenes, one answer booklet.

HOW TO IMPROVE YOUR SPEAKING AND LISTENING

Talking, discussing and sharing ideas are very useful ways to improve your understanding in other areas of English. Here are some ideas for improving your performance in some of the areas listed below.

ASKING QUESTIONS

This is an excellent way to improve your levels of understanding. Asking a question does not always mean that you don't understand what your teacher is talking about. If you do understand everything continue to ask questions. It allows you to look beneath the surface for less obvious meaning. You will be given credit for asking intelligent and searching questions.

ANSWERING QUESTIONS

You should always attempt to answer questions in group discussions or oral tests. Even if you get the answer wrong, you will be given credit for thinking and trying your best. If you don't feel sure of an answer you should still have a go. You may have approached the problem from another angle or thought of something that your teacher did not consider. It does happen!

INFORMAL DISCUSSION

You will often be asked to discuss work in small groups (not just in English). It might be a poem, a character's strengths and weaknesses, a new approach to a problem or a social issue. The key to success is to speak and listen. This will allow you to share information and develop new ideas before sharing them with a larger group. You will lose marks if you remain silent and just listen. You will also lose marks if you are aggressive or you talk too much and ignore the ideas of others.

ROLE PLAY

Take time to think about the main concerns and emotions of the character you are taking on. Think about the style of language your character would use: formal or informal, local slang or dialect, etc.

FORMAL DEBATE

There are rules and procedures to follow in a debate – your teacher will explain these to you. The important thing to remember is that you must use Standard English. Do not use slang, colloquialisms or dialect words. A debate is about listening to others as well as putting your own point across. You will develop a much stronger argument if you listen and respond to the points made by the opposition. Make sure that you listen to their points and respond to them as well as putting forward your arguments.

READING ALOUD

This is a skill that can only be developed with practice. Always speak clearly and stand or sit up straight. Read to the punctuation to maintain the sense of what you are reading. Think about the content of the piece you are reading. Try to express the emotions of the characters you are reading by varying the pace and tone of your voice.

Examiner's Top Tip
If you are not confident in Speaking and Listening then try to note down at least one point or question and make sure you use it in the debate or discussion.

TO ACHIEVE LEVEL 5 YOU NEED TO

- attempt to use Standard English in formal situations
- develop ideas and sequence events through talk
- ask questions to develop ideas
- listen carefully to the opinions and ideas of others

Examiner's Top Tip

L7: If you are confident about speaking in a group, then help others by asking supportive questions to bring in a weaker member of your group or by reinforcing a point made by somebody else.

TO MOVE FROM LEVEL 5 TO LEVELS 6 AND 7 YOU ALSO NEED TO

- make fluent and confident use of Standard English in formal situations
- extend your vocabulary
- listen and respond with sensitivity to the ideas of others
- engage the interest of your listener by varying pace, tone and style of presentation
- show an awareness of your audience by using appropriate language, tone and pace

SPEAKING & LISTENING

YOUR FINAL LEVEL FOR SPEAKING AND LISTENING IS DECIDED ON BY YOUR ENGLISH TEACHER. IT IS BASED ON YOUR PERFORMANCE OVER THE WHOLE OF YEAR 9.

TASKS YOU MIGHT EXPECT

- **answering questions in class**
- **asking questions in class**
- **informal paired discussion**
- **informal group discussion**
- **formal debate**
- **formal paired interviews on a specified topic**
- **giving a talk (formal or informal)**
- **reading aloud**
- **role play or drama.**

Have a go ...

1. Plan a talk on a subject you are interested in. Make a tape recording of your talk so you can work out how to improve your performance.
2. Choose a passage from your reading book and practise reading aloud at home.
3. Discuss your home-work, the news or recent events in your favourite scap opera with a friend or your family.

IMAGERY

Examiner's Top Tip
Try to use the correct technical terms when you are writing about literature.

Image: a picture painted with words. You may pick out a sensory image or an image of war, etc.

Metaphor: an assertion that one object is a completely different object – there is no comparison made. Similar effect to simile but much more powerful. E.g. His final words were icy splinters that lodged in her heart.

- Extended metaphor: a metaphor built up in a longer section of writing. The extended metaphor could be built using similes and other images.

Oxymoron: the joining of two words or phrases that appear to be complete opposites in meaning. E.g. Feather of lead, bright smoke, cold fire, sick health, Still waking sleep. (*Romeo and Juliet* Act 1, Scene 1). This emphasises Romeo's dissatisfaction and confusion. He loves Juliet, a Capulet; he should hate her.

Personification: an inanimate object is given human qualities or attributes. E.g. Well-apparell'd April on the heel/Of limping winter treads (*Romeo and Juliet* Act 1 Scene 2). This compares the seasons of spring and winter to a young lover and an old man near the end of his life.

Simile: a comparison of two distinctly different objects using the words like or as. Used to make particular associations in the mind of the reader. E.g. Some sat/poised like mud grenades (a description of frogs).

STRUCTURE

Caesura: a pause in the middle of line of poetry or a sentence in prose, for dramatic effect. E.g. Angry frogs invaded the flax-dam; I ducked through the hedges.

End-stopped line: in poetry, a full stop or colon at the end of a line that causes the reader to pause. This is sometimes used for dramatic effect, particularly when used with enjambment.

Enjambment: run-on lines – when the meaning of a line 'runs on' to the next line without any mark of punctuation. Often used to show movement or excitement in a poem.

Free verse: describes a poem that has a free structure, without a regular rhythm, rhyme scheme or stanza length.

Rhyme: the ending of one word sounds the same as another e.g. late/fate; sight/might; health/wealth.

- **End rhymes are most common. These are rhymes which occur at the end of a verse line.**
- **Internal rhymes occur in the middle of a line.**
- **Rhyme schemes are patterns of rhyme within a poem. Used for a variety of effects: to give structure; in comic verse; to link ideas.**

Rhythm: the pattern of beats or stresses in a line or group of lines.

Stanza: a verse – a group of lines in poetry.

Examiner's Top Tip
Don't just identify images or devices. You must explain why they are effective.

DEVICE

Alliteration: the repetition of a letter or letter sound at the beginning of a sequence of words. Used for emphasis and to link ideas. E.g. The silver snake slithered silently by.
Assonance: the repetition of identical or similar vowel sounds in a sequence of words. E.g. Silent, quiet, light, time (long 'i' sound).
Onomatopoeia: the sound of a word reflects the sound that it describes. E.g. plop, hiss, fizz, splash.

A GLOSSARY OF LITERARY TERMS

USE THIS GLOSSARY AS YOU WORK THROUGH THE FOLLOWING CHAPTERS IN THIS BOOK.

OTHER TERMS

Empathy: writers put themselves in the place of the person or object they are writing about; a stronger sensation than sympathy. If you empathise with someone you can understand how they feel and feel their pain, sadness, relief, etc. yourself.
Narrative: a story, whether told in prose or poetic form.

- First-person narrative: events are narrated by a person involved in the story. E.g I walked along the hard, stony ground.
- Third-person narrative: events are narrated by an outside observer of the story. E.g. He walked along the hard, stony ground.

Narrator: the storyteller. Again you could have first- or third-person narrators.

PLOT

A well-constructed story-line will keep readers interested as they are keen to know how a story will develop. Many novels have sub-plots: minor story-lines that develop with the main plot. In a short extract it is only possible to work out what is happening at the time – you cannot comment on plot development.

Examiner's Top Tip
Although all of these elements are essential to fiction, authors will often give more weight to one feature than to others.

CHARACTERISATION

Writers try to know their characters very well – this helps to make them believable to the reader. We need to know what a character looks like; how they speak and behave; how they think and feel; how they get on with other characters. To maintain the flow of the plot it is not possible for a writer to directly tell us all of this information and so it is important to read beneath the surface for character development.

READING FICTION

Fiction is stories describing imaginary events and people.
Key ingredients in good fiction are:

- **plot**
- **characterisation**
- **relationships**
- **setting**
- **use of language**

This section will help you to identify these elements and make a personal response to fiction texts.

Examiner's Top Tip
Remember to identify and explain the effective use of these elements.

RELATIONSHIPS

We all have relationships – with family, friends, teachers or work colleagues. To be believable, fictional characters must develop relationships within a text. The development of a relationship can often be the central element of the plot.

SETTING

The setting of a piece of fiction, both in time and place, is very important. Setting can often be central to creating a particular atmosphere or reflecting the mood of a character.

USE OF LANGUAGE

Interesting use of language is what makes us keep on reading. To comment on the use of language in fiction you need to recognise the use of particular devices and structures, and the extent of the detail and description. Effective use of language will ensure that all of the other elements are brought to life. When thinking about language in fiction you should consider:

- choice of vocabulary
- adjectives
- adverbs
- sentence structure
- imagery – simile, metaphor, personification, etc.

Basic Questions

To help organise your thoughts, ask yourself four basic questions:

1. What is the story-line?
2. Who are the main characters?
3. What is their relationship?
4. Where is it set?

UNDERSTANDING FICTION

To achieve level 5 you need to:

- recognise what the characters are like
- have a general understanding of the whole text
- begin to read beneath the surface for meaning
- note the effect of particular words and phrases

To move from level 5 to levels 6 and 7 you also need to:

- comment on the writer's use of language
- comment on the structure of the text
- comment on the creation of setting and atmosphere
- recognise what the writer is trying to achieve and how they do this
- trace the development of plot, character and relationships
- give a personal response to the text.

EXAMPLE TEXT

I'M THE KING OF THE CASTLE BY SUSAN HILL

In this extract the boy, Kingshaw, has gone for a walk in the fields and has a very frightening experience.

Look for the ingredients:

- plot
- characterisation
- relationships
- setting
- use of language

See pages 13–14 where the text is explained.

THE TEXT

Extract from *I'm the King of the Castle* by Susan Hill

1 When he first saw the crow he took no notice. There had been several crows. This one glided into the corn on its enormous, ragged black wings. He began to be aware of it when it rose up suddenly, circled overhead, and then dived, to land not very far away from him. Kingshaw could see the feathers on its head, shining black in between the butter-coloured cornstalks. Then it rose, and circled, and came down again, this time not quite landing, but flapping about his head, beating its wings and making a sound like flat leather pieces being slapped together. It was the largest crow he had ever seen. As it came down for the third time, he looked up and noticed its beak, opening in a screech. The inside of its mouth was scarlet, it had small glinting eyes.

2 Kingshaw got up and flapped his arms. For a moment, the bird retreated a little way off, and higher up in the sky. He began to walk rather quickly back, through the path in the corn, looking ahead of him. Stupid to be scared of a rotten bird. What could a bird do? But he felt his own extreme isolation, high up in the cornfield.

3 For a moment, he could only hear the soft thudding of his own footsteps, and the silky sound of the corn, brushing against him. Then there was a rush of air, as the great crow came beating down, and wheeled about his head. The beak opened and the hoarse caw came out again and again, from inside the scarlet mouth.

4 Kingshaw began to run, not caring, now, if he trampled the corn, wanting to get away, down into the next field. He thought that the corn might be some kind of crow's food store, in which he was seen as an invader. Perhaps this was only the first of a whole battalion of crows, that would rise up and swoop at him. Get on the grass then, he thought, get on to the grass, that'll be safe, it'll go away. He wondered if it had mistaken him for some hostile animal, lurking down in the corn.

????

What is the story-line?

????

Who are the main characters?

5 His progress was very slow, through the cornfield, the thick stalks bunched together and got in his way, and he had to shove them back with his arms. But he reached the gate and climbed it, and dropped on to the grass of the field on the other side. Sweat was running down his forehead and into his eyes. He looked up. The crow kept on coming. He ran.

6 But it wasn't easy to run down this field, either, because of the tractor ruts. He began to leap wildly from side to side of them, his legs stretched as far as they could go, and for a short time, it seemed that he did go faster. The crow dived again, and, as it rose, Kingshaw felt the tip of its black wing, beating against his face. He gave a sudden, dry sob. Then his left foot caught in one of the ruts and he keeled over, going down straight forwards.

7 He lay with his face in the coarse grass, panting and sobbing by turns, with the sound of his own blood pumping through his ears. He felt the sun on the back of his neck, and his ankle was wrenched. But he would be able to get up. He raised his head, and wiped two fingers across his face. A streak of blood came off, from where a thistle had scratched him. He got unsteadily to his feet, taking in deep, desperate breaths of the close air. He could not see the crow.

8 But when he began to walk forwards again, it rose up from the grass a little way off, and began to circle and swoop. Kingshaw broke into a run, sobbing and wiping the damp mess of tears and sweat off his face with one hand. There was a blister on his ankle, rubbed raw by the sandal strap. The crow was still quite high, soaring easily, to keep pace with him. Now, he had scrambled over the third gate, and he was in the field next to the one that belonged to Warings. He could see the back of the house, he began to run much faster.

9 This time, he fell and lay completely winded. Through the runnels of sweat and the sticky tufts of his own hair, he could see a figure looking down at him from one of the top windows of the house.

10 Then, there was a single screech, and the terrible beating of wings, and the crow swooped down and landed in the middle of his back.

11 Kingshaw thought that, in the end, it must have been his screaming that frightened it off, for he dared not move. He lay and closed his eyes and felt the claws of the bird, digging into his skin, through the thin shirt, and began to scream in a queer, gasping sort of way. After a moment or two, the bird rose. He had expected it to begin pecking at him with its beak, remembering terrible stories about vultures that went for living people's eyes. He could not believe in his own escape.

????	????
What is their relationship?	**Where is it set?**

PLOT

In this section the story is exciting and dramatic. It is a story of being chased or followed; it is told entirely from the victim's point of view so that the reader can identify closely with him. This section has a double build-up of tension. It builds up to paragraph 6 when the boy falls; we breathe a sigh of relief as the crow disappears. But then tension mounts when it reappears; there is a continued build-up to paragraph 9 when he falls again. This time it is worse because the crow lands on him.

Examiner's Top Tip
If you were writing about this text in an exam you would need to explain how each of these elements is effective.

THE TEXT EXPLAINED

- The writer is trying to create an atmosphere of tension and fear. To look at how this is achieved we should return to the basic elements of fiction described earlier.

Story-line: The boy, Kingshaw, is chased through a cornfield by a crow. He falls and the crow lands on his back. His screams finally scare it away.
Characters/relationship: Kingshaw and the crow; hunter (crow) and hunted (Kingshaw).
Setting: Isolated cornfields.

CHARACTERISATION

- The characterisation of the boy is important because it helps us understand why he is so frightened. He obviously has a powerful imagination: 'perhaps this was only the first of a whole battalion of crows' (paragraph 4). He is also presented as being sensitive to what people say and quite easily frightened: 'remembering terrible stories about vultures that went for living people's eyes' (paragraph 11).
- 'Stupid to be scared of a rotten bird. What could a bird do?' The tone of this suggests that he is angry with himself for being scared. Although he seems to be quite young he is aware of his weaknesses and is critical of them.

RELATIONSHIPS

The relationship between hunter and hunted is developed through the boy's fear. The power of the crow is increased through reference to its size: 'enormous, ragged black wings'; 'the largest crow he had ever seen'; 'the great crow'. There really isn't a relationship as such and this makes the boy seem very isolated.

SETTING

The setting is not the most important element in this piece of writing. The sense of menace is built up through the description of the crow rather than the surroundings. However, there is a sense that the landscape begins to turn against him: 'he felt his own extreme isolation'; 'thick stalks bunched together and got in his way'; 'it wasn't easy to run ... because of the tractor ruts'; 'a thistle scratched him'.

USE OF LANGUAGE

Examiner's Top Tip
A key point to think about is how the writer brings the crow to life.

The way that this section is written, the use of language and structure, is what makes it powerful.

DETAIL

There is extensive detail about the crow, making it seem more real. There is a description of what it sounds like as well as what it looks like. The detailed description of sounds made by the boy and the crow make the reader feel that there is a complete absence of background noise, highlighting his isolation: 'the sound of his own blood pumping through his ears.'

STRUCTURE

The paragraphs in this extract are all quite short; this keeps the story moving at a quick pace. Some sentences are particularly short; this is a device used by writers to build up dramatic tension and suspense: 'He looked up. The crow kept on coming. He ran.'

REPETITION

Minor details become more significant because they are repeated. For example: 'the inside of its mouth was scarlet' (paragraphs 1 and 3). The structure is repetitive: he runs away and falls, then the same thing happens again.

GLOSSARY

Remember to refer to the glossary of literary terms on pages 8–9.

FICTION TEST – Use the questions to test your progress. Check your answers on page 94.

FROM *A KESTREL FOR A KNAVE* BY BARRY HINES

In this extract Mr Sugden is angry with Billy as he believes he let a goal in deliberately at the end of the PE lesson. Billy is made to have a shower before he is allowed to go home.

A Kestrel for a Knave

He thought this was funny, Billy didn't. So Sugden looked round for a more appreciative audience. But no one was listening. They faced up for a few more seconds, then Billy turned back to his peg. He undressed quickly, bending his pumps free of his heels and sliding them off without untying the laces. When he stood up the black soles of his socks stamped damp imprints on the dry floor, which developed into a haphazard set of footprints when he removed his socks and stepped around pulling his jeans down. His ankles and knees were ingrained with ancient dirt which seemed to belong to the pigmentation of his skin. His left leg sported a mud stripe, and both his knees were encrusted. The surfaces of these mobile crusts were hair-lined, and with every flexion of the knee these lines opened into frown-like furrows.

For an instant, as he hurried into the showers, with one leg angled in running, with his dirty legs and huge rib cage moulding the skin of his white body, with his hollow cheek in profile, and the sabre of shadow emanating from the eye-hole, just for a moment he resembled an old print of a child hurrying towards the final solution.

****

While he worked on his ankles and heels Sugden stationed three boys at one end of the showers and moved to the other end, where the controls fed into the pipes on the wall … The blunt arrow was pointing to HOT. Sugden swung it back over WARM TO COLD. For a few seconds there was no visible change in the temperature, and the red slice held steady, still dominating the dial. Then it began to recede, slowly at first, then swiftly, its share of the face diminishing rapidly.

The cold water made Billy gasp. He held out his hands as though testing for rain, then ran for the end. The three guards barred the exit.

'Hey up, shift! Let me out, you rotten dogs!' They held him easily so he swished back to the other end, yelling all the way along. Sugden pushed him in the chest as he clung his way round the corner.

'Got a sweat on, Casper?'

'Let me out, Sir. Let me come.'

'I thought you'd like a cooler after your exertions in goal.'

'I'm frozen!'

'Really?'

'Gi' o'er, Sir! It's not right!'

'And was it right when you let the last goal in?'

'I couldn't help it!'

'Rubbish, lad.'

Billy tried another rush. Sugden repelled it, so he tried the other end again. Every time he tried to escape the three boys bounced him back, stinging him with their snapping towels as he retreated. He tried manoeuvring the nozzles, but whichever way he twisted them the water still found him out. Until finally he gave up, and stood amongst them, tolerating the freezing spray in silence. When Billy stopped yelling the other boys stopped laughing, and when time passed and no more was heard from him, their conversations began to peter out, and attention gradually focused on the showers. Until only a trio was left shouting into each other's faces, unaware that the volume of noise in the room had dropped. Suddenly they stopped, looked round embarrassed,

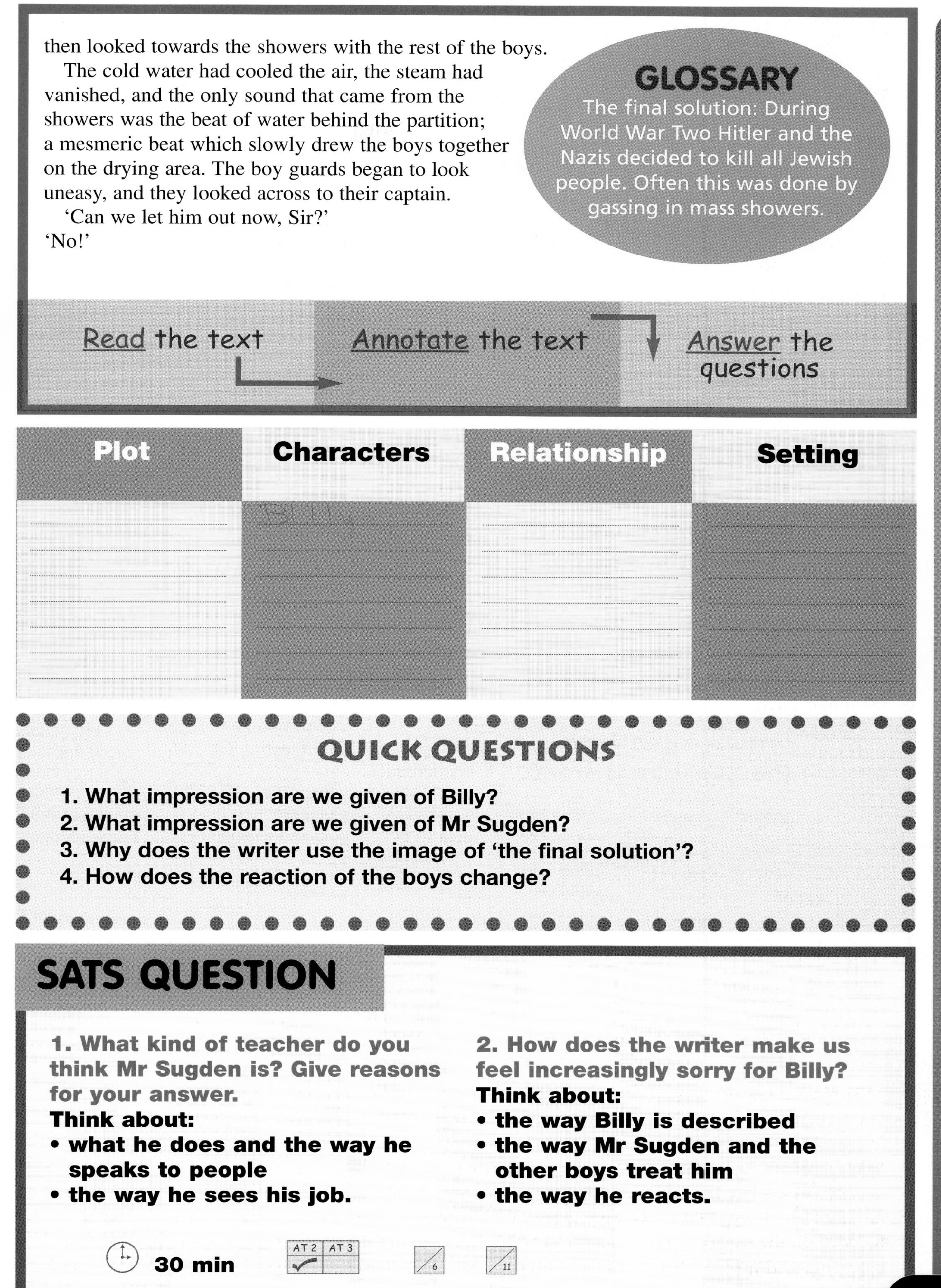

then looked towards the showers with the rest of the boys.

The cold water had cooled the air, the steam had vanished, and the only sound that came from the showers was the beat of water behind the partition; a mesmeric beat which slowly drew the boys together on the drying area. The boy guards began to look uneasy, and they looked across to their captain.

'Can we let him out now, Sir?'

'No!'

GLOSSARY

The final solution: During World War Two Hitler and the Nazis decided to kill all Jewish people. Often this was done by gassing in mass showers.

Read the text → Annotate the text → Answer the questions

Plot	Characters	Relationship	Setting
	Billy		

QUICK QUESTIONS

1. **What impression are we given of Billy?**
2. **What impression are we given of Mr Sugden?**
3. **Why does the writer use the image of 'the final solution'?**
4. **How does the reaction of the boys change?**

SATS QUESTION

1. What kind of teacher do you think Mr Sugden is? Give reasons for your answer.

Think about:
- **what he does and the way he speaks to people**
- **the way he sees his job.**

2. How does the writer make us feel increasingly sorry for Billy?

Think about:
- **the way Billy is described**
- **the way Mr Sugden and the other boys treat him**
- **the way he reacts.**

30 min

AT 2	AT 3
✓	

/6 /11

WHAT TO EXPECT

- Many students think they 'can't do poetry' – they worry about it, perhaps because it is less familiar than other forms of writing. We feel comfortable with fiction, advertising and newspaper reports because we see them around us all the time.
- When trying to understand poetry, it is important to remember that it is simply another means of communicating. A poem is written by another human being wanting to communicate ideas, feelings, memories, hopes and dreams. It may seem less obvious than other forms of writing but this is just because poems are often more compact and less expansive than fiction, for example.

GLOSSARY
As you work through this section remember to refer to the glossary of literary terms on pages 8–9.

POETRY IN SATS

- **Your understanding of poetry might be tested in Section B of Paper One in your SATS.**
- **You will have 20–25 minutes to answer one question on one poem.**
- **The question tests your understanding and response to poetry, not your written expression.**
- **The question is worth 11 marks.**

AT 2	AT 3
✓	

/11

UNDERSTANDING A POEM

TO ACHIEVE LEVEL 5 YOU NEED TO:
- understand what the poem is about
- begin to look for layers of meaning beneath the surface of the text
- understand ideas and feelings in the poem
- notice the effects of particular words and phrases.

TO MOVE FROM LEVEL 5 TO LEVELS 6 AND 7 YOU ALSO NEED TO:
- comment on the effective use of words and phrases and particular devices of language
- locate and comment on the use of imagery
- comment on the structure of the poem
- trace development within a poem
- give a personal response to the poem and what you think the poet has achieved.

READING POETRY

By the end of this section you will be able to identify and comment on:

- **title**
- **poetic voice**
- **imagery**
- **language devices**
- **structure**

You should be able to use these elements to make a personal response to poetry.

READING THE POEM

- You shouldn't expect to understand everything about a poem after a first reading; it will be packed full of emotions, ideas and images. Reading a poem involves detective work – you have to look closely under the surface for clues.
- Try reading a poem through three times, each time looking for a different set of clues.

Examiner's Top Tip

Remember, just like a painting or a piece of music, a poem can be responded to in many different ways. So long as you can justify (back up and explain) your opinion you can't go wrong!

Have a go ...

Now read the poem by Seamus Heaney printed on the next page. Read it three times and look for the different clues each time. See if you agree with the ideas on the next page.

First reading: The general meaning and story-line of the poem (if it has one).

Second reading: Feelings and emotions contained in the poem.

Third reading: Interesting images contained in the poem.

DEATH OF A NATURALIST

meaning?

time → All year the flax-dam festered in the heart
Of the townland; green and heavy headed
Flax had rotted there, weighted down by huge sods.
Daily it sweltered in the punishing sun.
Bubbles gargled delicately, bluebottles
Wove a strong gauze of sound around the smell.
There were dragon-flies, spotted butterflies,
But best of all was the warm thick slobber
Of frogspawn that grew like clotted water
In the shade of the banks. Here, every spring
I would fill jampotsful of the jellied
Specks to range on window-sills at home,
On shelves at school, and wait and watch until
The fattening dots burst into nimble-
Swimming tadpoles. Miss Walls would tell us how
The daddy frog was called a bullfrog
And how he croaked and how the mammy frog
Laid hundreds of little eggs and this was
Frogspawn. You could tell the weather by frogs too
For they were yellow in the sun and brown
In rain.

Then one hot day when fields were rank
With cowdung in the grass and angry frogs
Invaded the flax-dam; I ducked through hedges
To a coarse croaking that I had not heard
Before. The air was thick with a bass chorus.
Right down the dam gross-bellied frogs were cocked
On sods; their loose necks pulsed like sails. Some hopped
The slap and plop were obscene threats. Some sat
Poised like mud grenades, their blunt heads farting.
I sickened, turned, and ran. The great slime kings
Were gathered there for vengeance and I knew
That if I dipped my hand the spawn would clutch it.

Seamus Heaney

Annotations: sensory images; simile; time; long sentence; voice; time; war image; onomatopoeia; simile; war image; short sentence; comic book image

Examiner's Top Tip
Making notes or annotating a poem (underlining and highlighting, etc.) is a helpful way of organising your thoughts about it.

1ST READING

The poem is about a young boy (the poet) interested in nature, particularly frogspawn; he collects it and watches it grow. One day he is frightened by the frogs; he imagines they are going to attack him. He runs away; this ends his interest in nature.

2ND READING

Stanza One: fascination with nature and wildlife; excitement waiting for hatching; fond memories of childhood
Stanza Two: fear of big frogs; revulsion at their appearance; terror and hatred

3RD READING

"bubbles gargled delicately"; "gauze of sound"; "clotted water"; images of war; "The great slime kings"

TIME

The references to time in this poem are very interesting. In the first stanza all the times are general: 'All year', 'every spring'. The first stanza describes a general interest in nature. It also shows that the collecting of frogspawn is something he does every year and that he is very familiar with the area he describes, having visited it often: 'Daily it sweltered...' The reference to time in the second stanza is a signpost for the move from general enjoyment to a specific event at a specific point in time: 'Then one hot day...'.

DEATH OF A NATURALIST: THE TEXT EXPLAINED

SIMILES

If you pick out similes you must also explain why they are effective. For example: 'poised like mud grenades'. This shows that the poet found them threatening and unpredictable, likely to explode (jump) at any time. It also reflects the colour and shape of the frogs.

WAR IMAGES

Notice the use of words connected to war in the second stanza. The young boy feels as though the frogs have formed an army to fight back against the theft of frogspawn. He feels as if he's about to be ambushed: 'I ducked through hedges'.

COMIC BOOK IMAGE

'The great slime kings' are the product of a young child's overactive imagination just like monsters that hide under your bed! Where the first stanza contained sophisticated language and images from adulthood, this seems to come straight out of a nightmare or a comic strip, reflecting the raw terror felt at the time. He doesn't think the spawn might clutch his hand, he knows.

ONOMATOPOEIA

Words like 'slap' and 'plop' give his writing immediacy because they make the reader feel as if they can hear the threatening sounds that the young boy heard.

Examiner's Top Tip

If you are using technical terms from the glossary, make sure you spell them correctly.

TITLE: DEATH OF A NATURALIST

The title is confusing; we expect to read about a death, instead we find the story of a young boy's fascination with frogspawn. As we read on we discover that the death is not literal (real), it is symbolic (represents something else).
A naturalist is a person who is interested in nature and wildlife, the young boy in this case; the death is of his interest in nature. After the encounter with the frogs he is no longer a naturalist.
This poem is about 'rites of passage', the move from childhood into adulthood.
The poem could also symbolise the 'death' of childhood innocence. The innocent view of the goodness of nature is destroyed, never to be regained.

POETIC VOICE

Most of the poem is written in voice of the poet remembering his youth, but lines 16–19 are the voice of Miss Walls, his primary school teacher. The change of voice adds variety and also shows that these words have stayed in his memory. The vocabulary is more childish; 'the mammy frog'. This provides a contrast to the more sophisticated language used earlier in the stanza, e.g. 'bubbles gargled delicately'.

SENSORY IMAGES

- This is an image that draws on one or more of your five senses (touch, taste, smell, sight and hearing). There are a number of sensory images in this poem. They are used to give the reader a sense of actually experiencing the same thing as the poet and sometimes to trigger 'sensory memories'. This sounds complicated but what it means is that if you have ever put your hand in frogspawn, the description should make you remember what it actually felt like.
- To move up a level (level 6/7), try to think of other reasons why sensory images may have been used. For example, he is writing about childhood experiences. Children learn through their senses – every new sound, smell and taste is remembered. The 'warm thick slobber/Of frogspawn' is, perhaps, connected to a memory of a dog licking a hand or face!
- Think about the language used to express these images. For example: 'bubbles gargled delicately' – this is not the language of a young child. It shows that this is a mature adult fondly remembering, perhaps romanticising, his past. You could perhaps try to explain the contradictions of 'gauze of sound' and 'clotted water'. Why did he use these images?

THE POEM EXPLAINED

You shouldn't feel daunted by such a detailed explanation of the poem. It covers most of the elements that you could pick out of the text. You would not be expected to write at such length.

SENTENCE STRUCTURE

- In the second stanza sentences are quite short, particularly the one highlighted: 'I sickened, turned, and ran.' Short sentences are used to build up dramatic tension and suspense. This sentence comes as the threats have built to a peak and the young boy decides to run away. This sentence is broken into even shorter units by the use of commas, giving a moment's pause for thought before each action. This use of short sentences is in contrast to the rambling 34-word sentence in the first stanza. To best understand the effect of the sentence which begins: 'Here, every spring' you should go back to it and read it out loud.
- You should be feeling slightly out of breath now! As you read that section of the poem you find yourself speeding up to fit all the words in before you run out of breath. This is intended to reflect the excitement and anticipation of 'watching and waiting' for the hatching of the frogspawn. It also copies the final burst into life described at the end of the sentence. The technique of enjambment keeps the poem moving forward rather than breaking up the action with unnecessary commas and full stops.

Examiner's Top Tip

Remember to read to the punctuation. In other words, only take a breath when there is a punctuation mark.

Examiner's Top Tip

Notice there is always discussion of the effectiveness of devices and images. A key difference between level 4 answers and higher level answers is the ability to locate devices and features and the ability to comment on their effectiveness.

ADVICE

Go back to the poem and the explanations and pick out those parts with which you feel most comfortable, then try to look for those elements in other poems that you read. Build up gradually, looking for different elements each time you read.

THE BASIC AREAS COVERED ARE:

- title
- imagery
- language devices
- poetic voice
- structure
- personal response

POETRY TEST – Use the questions to test your progress. Check your answers on page 94.

Blackberry Picking

Late August, given heavy rain and sun
For a full week, the blackberries would ripen.
At first, just one, a glossy purple clot
Among others, red, green, hard as a knot.
You ate the first one and its flesh was sweet
Like thickened wine: summer's blood was in it
Leaving stains upon the tongue and lust for
Picking. Then red ones inked up and that hunger
Sent us out with milk-cans, pea-tins, jam-pots
Where briars scratched and wet grass bleached our boots.
Round hayfields, cornfields and potato drills
We trekked and picked until the cans were full,
Until the tinkling bottom had been covered
With green ones, and on top big dark blobs burned
Like a plate of eyes. Our hands were peppered
With thorn pricks, our palms sticky as Bluebeard's.

We hoarded the fresh berries in the byre.
But when the bath was filled we found a fur,
A rat-grey fungus glutting on our cache.
The juice was stinking too. Once off the bush
The fruit fermented, the sweet flesh would turn sour.
I always felt like crying. It wasn't fair
That all the lovely canfuls smelt of rot.
Each year I hoped they would keep, knew they would not.

Seamus Heaney

GLOSSARY

Bluebeard: A pirate who killed many of his wives by chopping off their heads.
Byre: A cowshed.
Cache: A hidden store of treasure, provisions or weapons.

Read the poem three times → Annotate the poem → Answer the questions

1st READING
The story-line

2nd READING
Feelings and emotions in the poem

3rd READING
Interesting images and phrases

QUICK QUESTIONS

1. How are the words 'Bluebeard', 'hoarded' and 'cache' linked? Why did Heaney choose to use this image?
2. In the last three lines the tone of voice is different. Where does this voice come from and why is it effective?
3. Look at the section beginning 'then red ones inked up' and ending 'a plate of eyes'. Why is the sentence structure and choice of vocabulary effective?

SATS QUESTION

1. How does the poet recreate his memories of childhood in this poem?

Think about:

- **the way actions are described**
- **the emotions he felt**
- **the structure, imagery and vocabulary used in the poem**
- **whether you think it is an effective description of childhood**

20 min

AT 2	AT 3
✓	

/11

READING A NON-FICTION TEXT

There are many different types of non-fiction text and they all follow different rules and conventions. The main non-fiction types are:

- *instruction*
- *information*
- *persuasion*
- *recount*
- *explanation*
- *discursive.*

On this page you will find a brief description of the convention of each text.

INSTRUCTION

Purpose: to instruct how something should be done through a series of sequenced steps.

STRUCTURE
A statement of what is to be achieved.
List of materials and equipment.
Sequenced/chronological steps.
Sometimes a diagram or illustration.

LANGUAGE
Written in the imperative – tells you what to do.

INFORMATION

Purpose: to describe the way things are; to give information.

STRUCTURE
Information is clearly organised
Information is linked.
Examples are included.

LANGUAGE
Present tense
Written in the third person: he, she, it

UNDERSTANDING NON-FICTION

TO ACHIEVE LEVEL 5 YOU NEED TO:

- find information and ideas in a text
- show a basic understanding of the text
- note the use of particular words and phrases
- be aware of why a text has been written.

TO MOVE FROM LEVEL 5 TO LEVELS 6 AND 7 YOU ALSO NEED TO:

- comment on use of language and layout (if appropriate)
- show awareness of what the writer is trying to achieve and how they do it
- say how successful you think the writer has been
- give a personal response to the text.

PERSUASION

Purpose:
to persuade or to argue the case for a point of view

STRUCTURE

Opening statement: E.g. vegetables are good for you.
Persuasive argument – point plus support.
Summary of argument and restatement of opening.

LANGUAGE

Present tense
Logical connectives

RECOUNT

Purpose: to retell event

STRUCTURE

An opening which sets the scene.
Events are retold in chronological order.

LANGUAGE

Written in the past tense
Uses temporal connectives: then, next, after
Focuses on individuals or groups of people: I, we

Examiner's Top Tip
When you are writing a non-fiction text make sure you follow these conventions.

Examiner's Top Tip
These conventions are not a rigid set of rules – they are intended as a guide. Many texts are mixed text types.

EXPLANATION

Purpose: to explain the process involved in natural and social phenomena or to explain how something works.

STRUCTURE

A statement to introduce the topic.
A series of logical steps explaining how and why something happens.
Steps continue until explanation is complete.

LANGUAGE

Present tense
Logical connectives:
this shows, because
Temporal connectives:
then, next, later

DISCURSIVE

Purpose: to present arguments and information rom differing viewpoints.

STRUCTURE

Statement of the issue to be discussed.
Argument for plus supporting evidence.
Argument against plus supporting evidence.
Summary of arguments and recommendation.

LANGUAGE

Present tense
Logical connectives:
therefore, however

DESCRIBING MEMORIES

The spider diagram below is planning to answer the following question:

Describe a journey you remember well

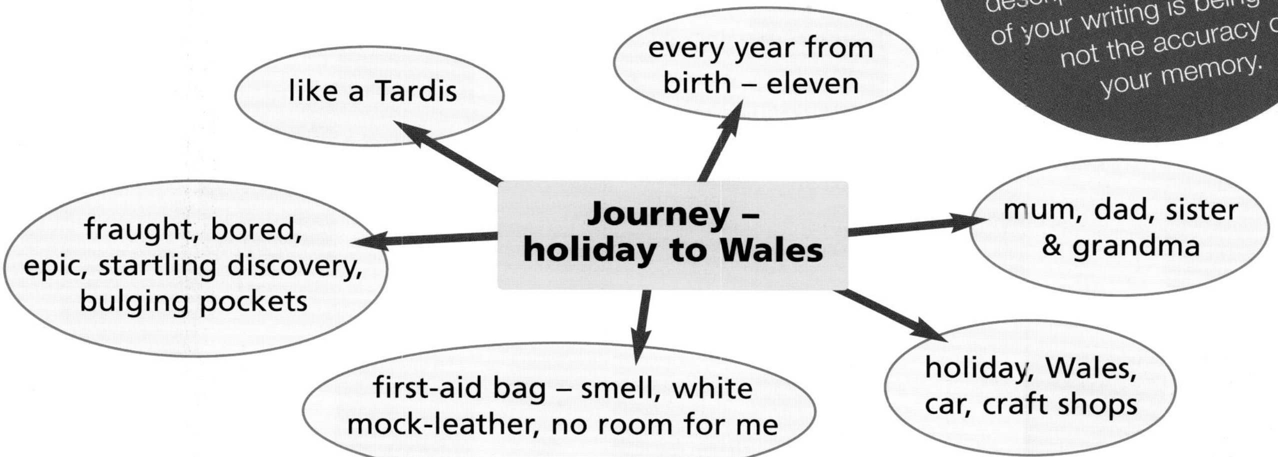

Journey – holiday to Wales

- like a Tardis
- every year from birth – eleven
- mum, dad, sister & grandma
- holiday, Wales, car, craft shops
- first-aid bag – smell, white mock-leather, no room for me
- fraught, bored, epic, startling discovery, bulging pockets

Examiner's Top Tip
It is perfectly acceptable to make up some or all of the details in a piece of descriptive writing. The quality of your writing is being tested, not the accuracy of your memory.

Now look at how this planning has been used to start a piece of writing:

At the age of fourteen I made a startling discovery – I only lived two hours away from the North Wales seaside town that had been the scene of many a happy family holiday. The reason for my surprise? From birth I had taken that same epic journey every year and our previous record was seven hours! My grandma always came on holiday with us and she is not the best traveller. As a result of this, I am familiar with every public toilet and small tearoom on our route. Delightful as they are, if you miss them out of the grand tour it takes hours off the journey time!

Our preparation for the journey always reminded me of the old joke, "How many elephants can you fit into a Mini?" Answer: none if you're going on holiday with us! Every available inch of space, including the Tardis-like side pockets, was filled with bodies and essential beach-holiday equipment.

As I was the youngest and smallest I had to sit in the middle, sandwiched between my fraught mother and bored sister. I had to fold myself up, knees jammed under my chin. There wasn't any floor space because the first-aid kit took up all the room. The first-aid kit was a white, mock-leather, drawstring bag that smelt of mothballs and camphor. The smell of the bag always made me feel a bit sick, which was unfortunate considering its purpose.

- dramatic choice of vocabulary to draw the reader in
- rhetorical question, involves the reader
- shorter sentence contrasts with the longer descriptive sentences
- vocabulary choice
- inclusion of humour
- simile
- adjective choices
- extended noun phrase to make the sentence more interesting
- sensory memory
- object detail

BELIEVABLE CHARACTERS

If the characters in your stories are to be convincing you need to know them before you start writing. Making a character fact file is an effective way to do this.

HAVE A GO NOW...

Name:

Age:

Occupation:

Appearance:

Personality:

Leisure/hobbies:

Ambition:

Fears:

Family:

Past/secret:

IMAGINATIVE WRITING:

MAKING YOUR WRITING MORE INTERESTING

To keep your writing interesting you need to think about how to:

- **create believable characters**
- **create different atmospheres**
- **use language to create particular effects.**

Examiner's Top Tip

When you are preparing for the SATS you should focus on different elements of your writing when you are attempting practice questions. Concentrate on structure, language, plot development, characterisation and accuracy.

CREATING ATMOSPHERE

elements are:

- the setting
- the way a character behaves
- use of language devices
- sentence structure
- vocabulary choices.

If you wanted to create a frightening atmosphere you might include some of the following ideas:

Setting: city at night, forest, beach during winter, castle or unoccupied building

Character behaviour: nervous, jumpy

Language devices: shadows danced like demented spirits

Sentence structure: short sentences and repetition

Vocabulary: isolated, deserted, gloomy, dank, murky

USING LANGUAGE

Examiner's Top Tip
When you read fiction at home and at school try to identify the techniques used by the author and think about how you could use similar devices in your own writing.

ADJECTIVES AND ADVERBS

Make use of descriptive words to make your writing interesting. For example, He sat down at the table.(simple sentence) Wearily, he sat down at the old, worn table. (the same sentence including a noun phrase)

COLOURS

Using colour in your descriptions can make them more interesting, especially if you try to be more adventurous than using yellow, red, blue, etc.
Here is a list of colours used by Susan Hill in the extract you read earlier: 'ragged black wings; butter-coloured corn stalks; its mouth was scarlet; the tip of its black wing'.

IMAGERY

Use similes, metaphors and personification in your writing.

SENSES

Include images or descriptions that will appeal to the five senses. For example, 'wiping the damp mess of tears and sweat off his face with one hand'. (*I'm the King of the Castle* by Susan Hill)

SENTENCE STRUCTURE

- Try to vary the length and construction of your sentences. This will make your writing more interesting. It will also allow you to use sentence structure for effect. If you have been writing fairly complex sentences, then a sudden change to short, simple sentences could show sudden fear.
- Here is another extract from Susan Hill's writing: 'Sweat was running down his forehead and into his eyes. He looked up. The crow kept on coming. He ran.'
- She could have written: 'He looked up and saw that the crow kept on coming so he ran.' All the dramatic tension is lost in this version.

CONVINCING DIALOGUE

Re-read this conversation from *A Kestrel for a Knave*. You read a longer extract in the Fiction Test (pages 16–17). Think about what we learn about the characters from this dialogue.

'Got a sweat on Casper?'
'Let me out, Sir. Let me come.'
'I thought you'd like a cooler after your exertions in goal.'
'I'm frozen!'
'Really?'
'Gi'o'er, Sir! It's not right!'
'And was it right when you let that last goal in?'
'I couldn't help it!'
'Rubbish, lad.'

1. The exclamation marks show that Billy is in pain or discomfort.

2. Mr Sugden's final comment shows that he thinks Billy is a liar.

3. Notice that the conversation is written as these people would really speak. 'Gi'o'er' is how Billy would say 'Give over'. Billy doesn't speak in Standard English – this style of writing indicates Billy's dialect and accent.

4. The conversation isn't always written in complete sentences because we don't always speak in complete sentences.

5. The whole conversation shows that Mr Sugden is more powerful than Billy.

I SAID, HE SAID, SHE SAID ...

- Notice that the example above doesn't use any speech descriptors (verbs) – he said, Billy shouted.
- When you use dialogue in a story think about all the different ways there are to describe how somebody says something. Using a variety of speech descriptors gives the reader more information about what a character is like.
- Here are some words you could use to replace said:

Have a Go...
Decide on a speech descriptor for each line in the conversation above. Choose from the list or use your own ideas.

WRITING CONVINCING DIALOGUE AND EXTENDING YOUR VOCABULARY

Dialogue is another word for speech or conversation. Most fiction contains dialogue because it allows the main characters to communicate with each other. Dialogue is important for the following reasons:

- it helps to bring the characters to life
- it reveals new information about the character speaking or the character being spoken about
- it adds variety to the story.

It is important to think about how characters say things as well as what they say.

THAT'S NICE

- In order to achieve level 5 you have to make use of interesting words and phrases. Think about how you can extend your vocabulary by replacing everyday words with something a little more imaginative.
- Instead of nice how about:

great, amazing, breath-taking, beautiful, attractive, superb, lovely, fine, excellent, magnificent

Examiner's Top Tip

In the National Curriculum orders, writing at level 5 is described as: 'varied and interesting … vocabulary choices are imaginative.'

THAT'S REALLY NICE...

Some words are more powerful than others. Your choice of vocabulary should also take account of how strong a word is. What order would you put these words and phrases in?

really nice
absolutely fantastic
quite good
satisfactory
appalling
very entertaining
reasonably satisfied

warm
hot
scorched
boiling
tepid
balmy
fiery

Have a go ...

Think of five alternatives for each of the following words. Try to put them in order according to how powerful each word is.

scared
excited
run
fall
angry
cold

IMAGINATIVE WRITING – STRUCTURE

Your writing needs clearly defined structure. This will usually take the form of three definite stages: the beginning, the middle and the ending.

THE BEGINNING

- In the opening section of a piece of imaginative writing, you need to introduce the characters and the setting, and begin to develop the main plot strands.
- It is important to create an interesting opening, as you need to capture the attention of your reader.
- Do not give your reader too much detail. Keep them guessing so that they will want to read on. Never launch straight into 'telling a story'.
- Begin with an interesting description of a character or the setting.
- If you are writing in first-person narrative, you could begin with an intriguing statement from your main character.

THE MIDDLE

- In the central section of your writing you need to develop plot, characterisation and relationships. Development is essential if you are to hold the interest of the reader.
- Make sure you keep a balance between dialogue (conversation) and description. Too much dialogue makes your writing stilted. (Remember you are not writing a script!)
- If you made a character fact file as preparation, make sure you introduce some details from it.
- Refer back to your character plan to make sure they react to events in the way their personality suggests. If you have said they are selfish and self-obsessed, they wouldn't offer a stranger help.
- Think about how you can use language and structure to make your writing interesting and lively.

THE ENDING

In the final section of your writing, you must begin to tie up loose ends. You have three main options for finishing your writing:

Cliffhanger: The story ends without conclusion or resolution. This keeps the reader guessing as to what will happen next. However, you need to leave some clues and have some ideas yourself for what will happen next. You should plan to finish in this way rather than realising you have run out of time. An unfinished ending and a cliffhanger ending are two completely different things.

Twist in the tale: A completely unexpected twist in the plot right at the end. This is an exciting way to end a story but it is also more difficult to manage. Again, it is important to plan for this kind of ending.

Resolution: All the loose ends are tied up and the ending is complete and definite. This would often be a happy ending but it doesn't have to be.

Try to avoid clichéd endings: You could really ruin a good story for want of an original conclusion. For example avoid, 'Then I woke up. It had all been a dream!'

Have a Go...

Plan the structure for a story about a journey to a new and unfamiliar place:

- Write the opening sentence.
- Decide on which kind of ending you will use.
- Write five main bullet points for each section.
- Think about: characters, setting, plot developments, relationship developments and language.

Examiner's Top Tip

If you can handle a more complicated structure, you could begin the story with the climax of the plot and go on to look at how the events took place. You could produce a circular structure by returning to the same event at the end.

Examiner's Top Tip

Time spent planning is time well spent. You should take between five and ten minutes to think about what you are going to write and how you are going to sustain your narrative.

GOOD NON-FICTION

To produce a good piece of non-fiction writing you need to have a clear sense of purpose. You need to know what you are trying to achieve as an end result. Usually it will be one of the following:

- **communicate information or ideas**
- **persuade people to buy something, take part in something or change their opinion about something**
- **express your own opinion.**

In every situation you will be targeting a specific audience. You need to keep that at the front of your mind when you write. Hopefully, this will help you to keep your writing direct and focused.

WRITING NON-FICTION

In the writing section of the SATS you may be required to write in one of the following styles. Writing to:

- explain
- inform
- persuade/argue
- describe (covered in the previous section).

Students tend to feel less confident with these forms of writing. Again this is because they tend to have less experience of them.

WHAT YOU HAVE TO DO

In the SATS you have approximately 40 minutes to complete an imaginative task or a non-fiction task. You would probably expect to produce between two and three sides of imaginative writing. However, all too often students produce just half a side of writing for the other tasks. Non-fiction writing is not an easy option and it also requires a detailed response.

Examiner's Top Tip

Often you will be asked to complete a writing task that is related to the reading section of the exam paper. You can use information from other sections of the paper in the writing task.

To achieve level 5 you need to:

- organise your ideas in a clear way
- interest and persuade your reader
- make use of a formal style and Standard English where appropriate
- support your ideas with evidence, examples and quotations
- begin to develop some of your ideas fully.

To move from level 5 to levels 6 and 7 you also need to:

- make use of particular language devices for effect
- use structure to create effects
- show an awareness of the audience and purpose you are writing for.

Examiner's Top Tip

You will find the main purpose and conventions of each text type on pages 26–27.

Basic questions

In the Reading Non-fiction and Media sections of this book, you were advised to ask yourself four basic questions after reading a text. When you write a non-fiction piece, you should be able to apply those same questions to your own work. If the answers are clear then you have done a good job. Those questions are:

Who is it aimed at?

Why has it been written?

What is the main idea/message in the text?

How is that message put across?

TASKS YOU MIGHT EXPECT

	Inform	Explain	Persuade/argue
Letter	✓	✓	✓
Leaflet	✓	✓	✓
Advertisement	✓		✓
Magazine article	✓	✓	✓ ✓
Talk	✓	✓	✓ ✓
Discursive essay			✓

WRITING A FORMAL LETTER

There are many reasons why you may need to write a formal letter. For example: to apply for a job; to complain to a company; to apply for a membership; to book a service or to request permission.

There are a lot of conventions to follow when you are writing a formal letter.

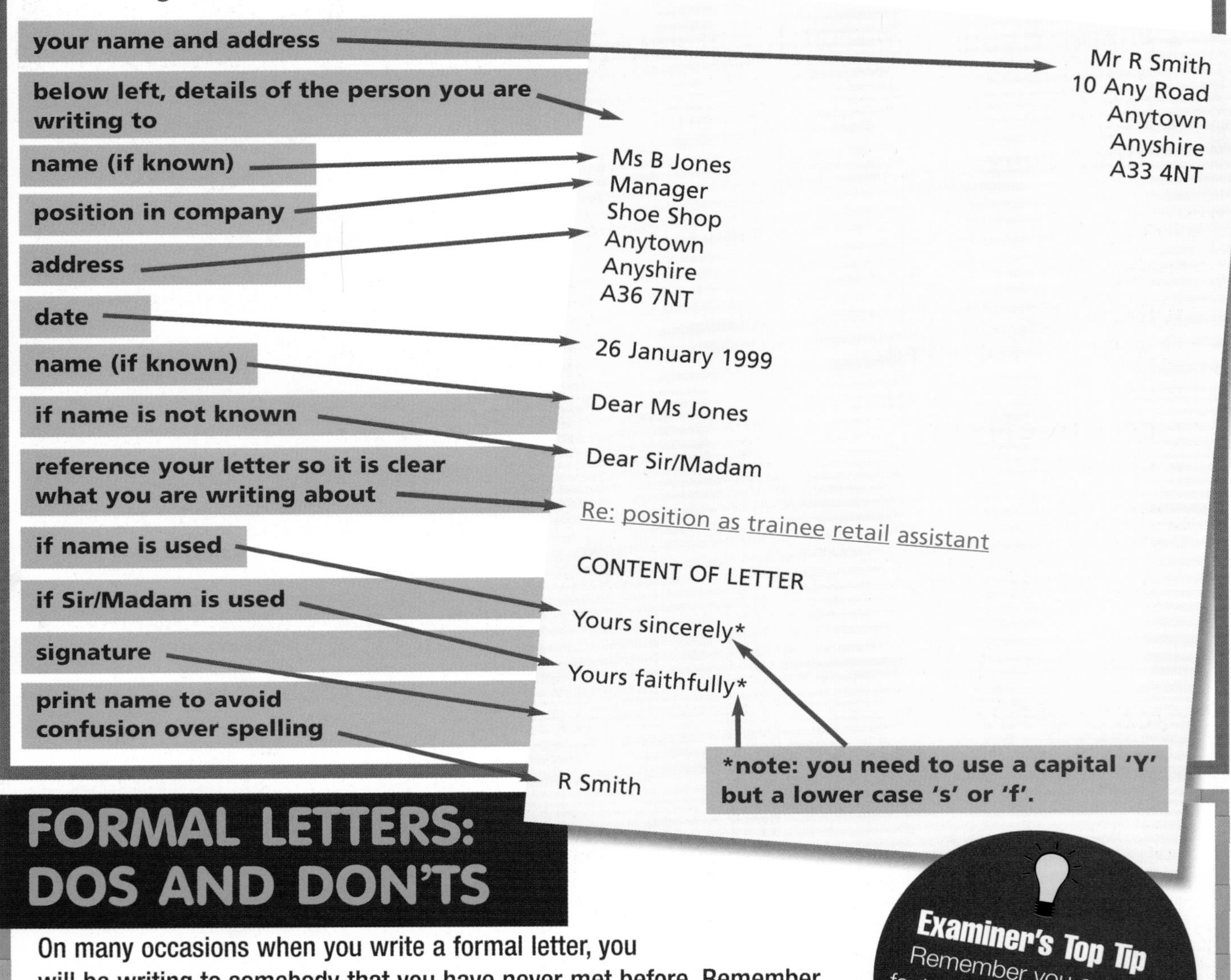

FORMAL LETTERS: DOS AND DON'TS

On many occasions when you write a formal letter, you will be writing to somebody that you have never met before. Remember the following points:

- Do use Standard English
- Don't use slang or conversational language
- Try not to be either aggressive or over-familiar in your tone
- Get to your point quickly and stick to your point.

If you choose a letter-writing task in the exam, you will not be required to write as much as an imaginative response. This means that you have plenty of time to plan the content, structure and accuracy of your letter. If you were applying for a job, you could include the following information (remember you are trying to persuade someone):

- an opening statement about why you want the job
- qualifications
- experience – the skills you have to do the job
- personal qualities – how your personality would suit you to the job
- why you want to work for that company.

Examiner's Top Tip
Remember you can use facts and phrases from the reading material in the other sections of the exam.

WRITING LETTERS

WRITING AN INFORMAL LETTER

If you are writing to a friend then the layout of your letter can be more informal. However, there are still some conventions you should follow.

10 Any Road
Anytown
Anyshire
A33 4NT

16th April 2001

Dear James,

CONTENT OF LETTER

Best wishes,

Jane

- **your address**
- **date**
- **first name of the person you are writing to**
- **you can use a range of 'complimentary close' phrases depending on how well you know the person**
- **Your name/signature**

Examiner's Top Tip
You may be asked to write a letter to inform, explain or persuade. Make sure you read the question carefully and write for the correct purpose.

INFORMAL LETTERS: DOS AND DON'TS

When you write an informal letter, you will be addressing somebody that you know well. Therefore, it is acceptable to use slang or conversational language. However, in an exam it would be advisable to write most of the letter in Standard English.

In an exam situation you should plan the content and structure of your letter. Think about all the topics you want to cover and decide on the best order to cover them so that your writing flows.

Remember, you will be instructed to write to inform or persuade your friend of something.

WRITING MEDIA TEXTS

The main media text types you could be asked to write are:

- leaflets
- advertisements
- magazine/newspaper articles

A good way to learn how to write in this style is to study examples of the style. Re-read the media sections of this book. The glossary on pages 38–39 explains the technical terms.

LEAFLETS

- **Leaflets are usually free and are often handed out or posted through your door at home. For this reason it is important to make an immediate visual impact through the use of pictures or bold, eye-catching headings.**
- **Information, advice or opinion needs to be presented in a clear and concise way.**
- **Information in leaflets needs to appear to be directed at the individual reader. For this reason you should use personal pronouns.**

LAYOUT AND PRESENTATION

The main devices you would use in a leaflet are:

- **bullet points**
- **columns**
- **pictures**
- **short paragraphs**
- **headings**

Have a Go...

Write five bullet points about the disadvantages of smoking, aimed at teenagers.

1. ....
2. ....
3. ....
4. ....
5. ....

Think of two presentational devices you might use in a leaflet to persuade teenagers to give up smoking.

1. ....
2. ....

Think of two pictures you could use in the same leaflet.

1. ....
2. ....

Examiner's Top Tip
If you want to include pictures in a leaflet simply draw a box and write what the picture would be.

ADVERTISEMENTS

As advertising relies so heavily on pictures, it is unlikely that you would be required to write an advertisement in your exam.

Some leaflets have an advertising function as well as offering advice or information.

Advertising language is very persuasive. If you were asked to design an advert you should think about the following:

- **emotive and persuasive language**
- **devices such as alliteration, repetition, puns and questions**
- **how to present opinions in a factual way.**

LAYOUT AND PRESENTATION

The main devices you would use are:

- **pictures**
- **different font styles and sizes.**

The main points to remember when you are writing a media text are:

- the purpose is usually to persuade although it could also be to advise or to inform
- clever use of language is essential
- you want people to remember your main message
- you need to be concise and precise
- layout and presentational devices are essential.

Have a go ...

- Think of a new product name and slogan for a box of chocolates.
- Write appealing descriptions of the following chocolates from your new range.

  Strawberry cream
  Caramel
  Dark chocolate and hazelnut
  Orange fondant

....
....
....
....
....
....
....
....

MAGAZINES/NEWSPAPERS

- News articles report something that has already happened so you must always write in the past tense.
- News articles usually report the most dramatic part of an event first and then retell the rest of the story in chronological order.
- News articles are written in Standard English. The only exception to this is direct quotation, which will be written exactly as the person said it.

LAYOUT AND PRESENTATION

The main devices you would use are:

- pictures
- columns
- short paragraphs
- headlines.

Have a Go...

- Write a headline and topic sentence about a lottery winner for a local newspaper.
- Think of two people you would interview for your article.
- Think of a photograph you would want for the story and write a caption to go with it.

....
....
....
....
....
....
....
....
....

Examiner's Top Tip

Remember: it is the quality of your writing that is being tested. Don't spend all your time colouring in.

WRITING ESSAYS

This is the most formal style of writing you will be required to use in the SATS. There are three different styles of essay you could be asked to write.

- argument
- discursive essay
- criticism.

Whilst it is possible to avoid this style of writing in Paper One you must write a literary criticism essay in Paper Two.

ARGUMENT

A one-sided essay expresses your own opinions about an issue. It should be structured as follows:

- Introduction explaining the issue and giving your opinion.
- A series of paragraphs to express the main points of your argument. You should include evidence to support your ideas. It is essential that you have a clear argument running through your essay. You should organise your points so that one builds on the next. Make sure you order your points to have the most impact.
- Conclusion summing up your main points and restating your opinion.

EXAMPLE INTRODUCTION

At present it is compulsory to wear a uniform at my school. A variety of reasons have been given for this rule and most parents think that it is a good idea. However, the uniform is uncomfortable and unfashionable; therefore, I believe students should be allowed to wear whatever they want. There are many strong arguments to support my point of view that uniform should be a thing of the past.

DISCURSIVE ESSAY

A discursive or balanced essay considers two sides of an issue. It should be structured as follows:

- Introduction explaining the issue.
- An organised series of paragraphs with points in favour of the issue.
- An organised series of paragraphs with points against the issue.
- Conclusion summing up the points for and against and giving your own opinion.

Have a Go...

Write a paragraph plan to continue the school uniform argument. Think of at least five main points with supporting evidence.

CONNECTIVES WORD BANK

When you write an essay giving your own opinion or that of others, you should always explain or support your argument. The words and phrases below will help you to do this.

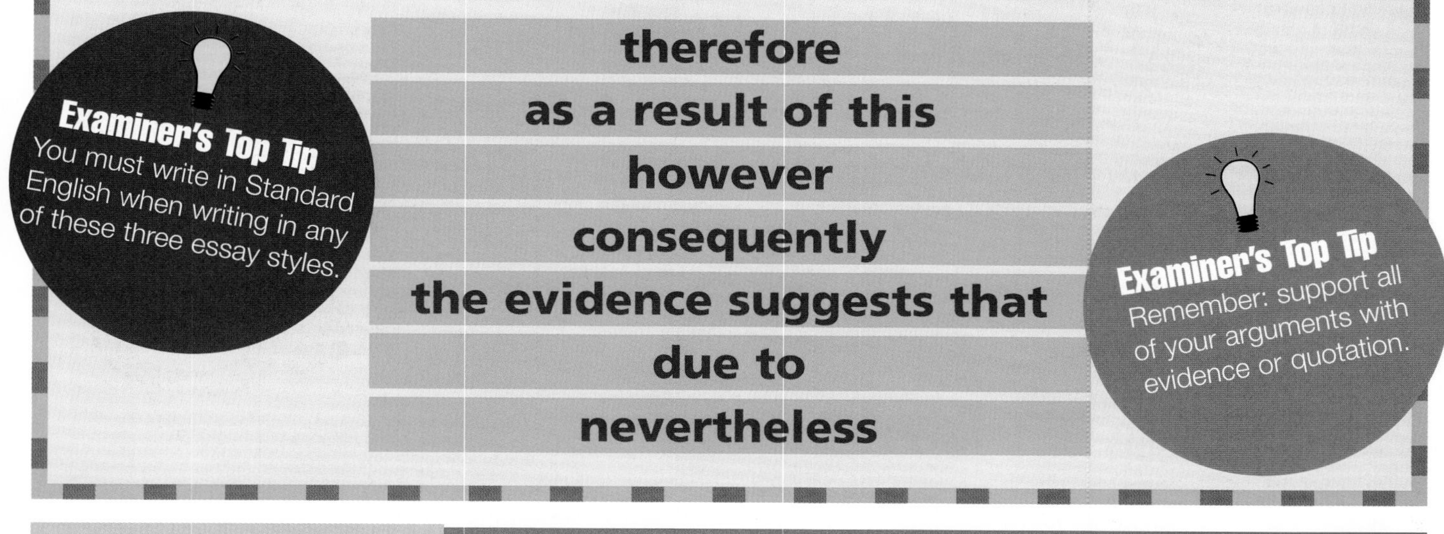

CRITICISM

Literary criticism is a style of writing that examines literature and explores how and why a text has been written, as well as how successful it has been. Criticism does not necessarily mean saying something is not very good. You can have a very positive critical opinion of a piece of writing.

You will use this style of writing in the Reading and Shakespeare sections of the SATS.

Your essay should be structured as follows:

- Introduction referring to the question. Make sure that your introduction captures the attention of the reader and demonstrates your understanding of the question.
- A series of paragraphs exploring different aspects of the question. Each point you make should be supported by relevant quotation or textual evidence.
- Conclusion drawing together the main points of your argument and referring back to the question.

WRITING TEST

You will be assessed on:
- **your ideas and the way you organise and express them**
- **your ability to write clearly, using paragraphs and accurate grammar, spelling and punctuation.**

1. IMAGINATIVE WRITING

Remember the basic ingredients for fiction:

- **plot/storyline**
- **characterisation**
- **relationships**
- **setting**
- **descriptive language and dialogue**

Examiner's Top Tip
Spend at least five minutes planning your answer.

1. 'It wasn't me!'
   Write about someone wrongly suspected or accused of committing a crime.
   Think about:
   - What they have been accused of.
   - How that person would feel.

2. Write about a frightening encounter with an animal.
   - Try to build up a feeling of tension or suspense.
   - Describe the animal.

3. Write about being lost or followed in a forest.
   - Try to build up an atmosphere of fear.
   - Describe the forest.
   - Write in the first or third person.

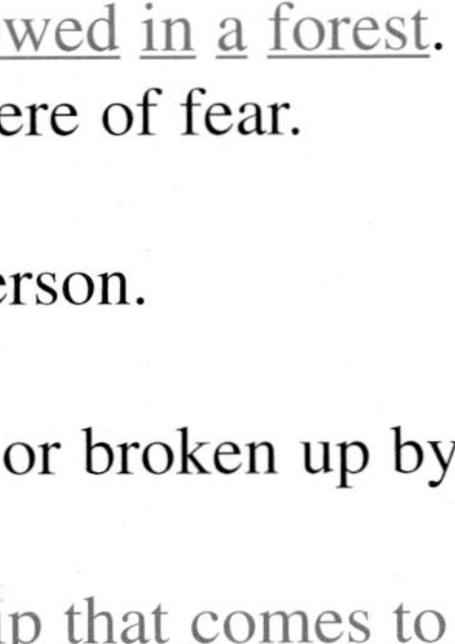

4. Relationships can be changed or broken up by many things, for example, a move away, death or an argument.
   Write about a close relationship that comes to an end.
   - Describe the relationship.
   - Explain why the relationship ended.
   - Try to recreate the emotions involved.

2. NON-FICTION WRITING

Remember the four basic questions to ask about a non-fiction text:

Who is it aimed at?	**Why has it been written?**
What is the main idea/ message in the text?	**How is that message put across?**

1. Imagine you are the director of a new museum.
   Write a letter to headteachers of schools in the area persuading them to bring groups of pupils to the museum.
   You could write about:
   - what the museum has to offer
   - why it is of educational value
   - how to organise a trip there.

2. Imagine you have been given a chance to give a talk to your class. Choose an issue you feel strongly about.
   Write a talk trying to persuade other people to support your views.

3. Describe a place you have enjoyed visiting.
   You could write about:
   - why you like it
   - any specific memories of the place
   - why you would recommend other people to visit this place.

4. Write a discursive essay about keeping animals in zoos and safari parks.
   Write about:
   - the points for keeping animals in captivity
   - the points against keeping animals in captivity
   - your own opinion.

5. Write an advice leaflet for teenagers preparing for exams. Think carefully about your presentation and layout.
   You should include:
   - advice and suggestions for revision
   - what to do in the exam
   - tips for relaxing.

Examiner's Top Tip
Remember: support all of your arguments with evidence or quotation.

40 min

AT 2	AT 3
	✓

/33

SHAKESPEARE

Paper Two of the SATS concentrates solely on your understanding of a Shakespeare play. There are three plays to choose from and your teacher will decide which one you are going to study. The plays are: *Macbeth*, *Henry V* or *Twelfth Night*.

TO ACHIEVE LEVEL 5 YOU NEED TO:

- show an understanding of the plot
- show some understanding of the feelings and behaviour of the characters
- note the effect of particular words and phrases
- show an understanding of how your scene fits into the play.

TO MOVE FROM LEVEL 5 TO LEVELS 6 AND 7 YOU ALSO NEED TO:

- support your ideas about characters and relationships with detailed reference to the text
- write in some detail about the effects of language
- show understanding of the more complex feelings of the characters
- show an awareness of how your scene is affected by events preceding it and how it affects the action that follows.

WHAT YOU WILL STUDY

- **There is a choice of two scenes from each play. Again, your teacher will decide which scene to concentrate on. Although you only need to study one scene in detail, you need to have some knowledge of the rest of the play.**
- **In the exam there will be one question relating to each scene. Your teacher will direct you to the correct question and scene.**

Examiner's Top Tip
You need to know your specified scene very well but you do not need to learn quotations. You will be provided with a copy of the scene with your exam paper.

WHAT YOU WILL BE TESTED ON

In Paper One, each section tests either Reading AT2 or Writing AT3. Paper Two tests both of these skills. You will be given two separate marks in this paper.

UNDERSTANDING AND RESPONSE

This covers your understanding of the scene and the whole play you have studied. Your understanding of and response to characters, relationships and plot development is assessed.

WRITTEN EXPRESSION

This assesses your ability to express meaning in your writing; the accuracy of spelling, punctuation and grammar is also tested.

EMPATHY/WRITING IN ROLE

You will be asked to imagine yourself to be a character in the scene and to write about how you feel about the events of the play you have been involved in. It is essential that you remain in role and refer to the character as 'I' or 'me'. For example, 'If I want to become king, I must kill Duncan.'
This type of question tests:

- your understanding of character emotions and reactions
- your understanding of plot development
- your ability to sustain writing in role.

LITERARY CRITICISM

You will be asked to write in a more detached way about:

- how characters behave
- how relationships are developed
- how atmosphere is created
- how language is used.

STAGING

You will be asked to write about how a scene should be performed on stage. This will test:

- **your understanding of key relationships**
- **your understanding of how language is used**
- **your ability to see the text as a piece for performance.**

Examiner's Top Tip

If you have studied the whole play by watching a film version, make sure you do not write about events that occur only in the film.

RHYME AND RHYTHM

Blank verse: unrhymed lines of iambic pentameter. Shakespeare wrote his plays in blank verse because it is versatile, it is not restricted by rhyme and it is the closest to the natural rhythms of speech. This makes it easy to create different moods – anger, love, etc.

Iambic pentameter: describes the number of syllables and stresses in a line, which is known as the meter. A foot is a pair of syllables. An iambic foot is an unstressed syllable followed by a stressed syllable. There are five iambic feet in iambic pentameter.

Canterbury:
It must / be so, / for mir / acles / are ceas'd,
And there / fore we / must needs / admit / the means,
How things / are per / fected./

(*Henry V* Act 1, Scene 1)

Examiner's Top Tip
If you are reading Shakespeare aloud try to read to the punctuation. This will help with the sense of what you are reading.

Rhyming couplets: sometimes Shakespeare wrote in different styles for contrast. More formal and traditional characters making important speeches may speak in rhyming couplets (the lines rhyme in pairs). Because of the constraint of finding rhymes there is less movement and freedom in these speeches. This reflects the characters' formality.

Capulet:
At my poor house look to behold this night
Earth-treading stars that make dark heaven light

(Romeo and Juliet)

Prose: the 'low characters', servants for example, speak in prose rather than verse. This reflects that they have less education and their subject matter is often low or coarse.

Sir Toby Belch:
Go, write it in a martial hand, be curst and brief; it is no matter how witty, so it be eloquent, and full of invention.

(*Twelfth Night* Act 3, Scene 2, lines 33–34)

Porter:
Marry, sir, nose-painting, sleep, and urine.

(*Macbeth* Act 2, Scene 3, line 27)

HOW TO READ SHAKESPEARE ALOUD

Shakespeare's language is always much easier to understand when it is read well. Follow these tips.

- **Read to the punctuation. If there is no punctuation at the end of a line then read straight through to the next line.**
- **Don't rush. Speak clearly and think about what you are saying.**
- **Words ending in 'd or –ed. If a word is spelt 'd, e.g. accus'd, you pronounce it as we would say accused. However, if it is spelt accused in the text you pronounce the -ed as a separate syllable – accuse-ed.**
- **Think about the tone of voice you should use.**
- **Think about what your character would do when saying the lines.**
- **Emphasise the words you think are most important. The natural stresses of iambic pentameter should help you to do this.**

UNDERSTANDING SHAKESPEARE'S LANGUAGE

The Shakespeare paper is the part of the test that causes most concern amongst students. Again, as with poetry, this is simply because it is less familiar and perhaps seems unconnected to modern-day concerns. However, Shakespeare's plays cover the same themes as any modern piece of writing: love, jealousy, ambition, family conflicts, murder and intrigue. Once the barriers of language have been broken down it is easy to see this.

THEE ... THOU ... WHO?

art	**are**	
hadst	**had**	
hence	**here**	
ill	**bad**	
o'er	**over**	
thee	**you**	
thou	**you**	**(used with someone very close to you or as an insult)**
you	**you**	**(a more distant way of speaking to someone)**

thy	**your**
whence	**where**
wither	**where**
wouldst	**would**

Examiner's Top Tip

Hearing Shakespeare's language read aloud helps you to understand the meaning. Try to see a live performance or a video version of the play you are studying.

12–16

The phrase 'double trust' emphasises that Macbeth would be breaking Duncan's trust twice. He sets out the reasons logically:

- **1a – he is his kinsman (relative)**
- **1b – he is a trusted subject**
- **2 – Duncan is a guest in his house so he should protect him, not plan to kill him. Macbeth presents himself with a well-reasoned argument against the murder plan.**

Examiner's Top Tip
If you pick out language devices you must explain how they are used and why they are effective.

16–18

These lines are more emotive. Macbeth reminds himself of all Duncan's qualities. Words like 'meek' and 'clear' are used to show that Duncan is virtuous and without sin.

18–19

Macbeth imagines that Duncan's virtues will call out like angels, with voices like trumpets. 'Trumpet-tongued' is a Homeric epithet; this is a compound of two words that defines a distinctive quality of a person or thing. In this case it represents a royal fanfare loudly blasting the news of the murder. The fact that the angels are 'trumpet-tongued' emphasises the fact that Duncan is without sin.

EXTRACT

He's here in double trust;
First as I am his kinsman and his subject,
Strong both against the deed; then as
his host,
Who should against his murderer
shut the door, 15
Not bear the knife myself. Besides this
Duncan
Hath borne his faculties so meek, hath
been
So clear in his great office, that his virtues
Will plead like angels, trumpet-tongued
against
The deep damnation of his taking-off 20
And pity, like a naked newborn babe
striding the blast, or heaven's cherubin
horsed
Upon the sightless couriers of the air,
Shall blow the horrid deed in every eye,
That tears shall drown the wind. I have
no spur 25
To prick the sides of my intent, but only
Vaulting ambition which o'erleaps itself
and falls on th'other –

Macbeth (Act 1, Scene 7, lines 1–28)

In this speech Macbeth lists all the reasons why he should not murder Duncan.

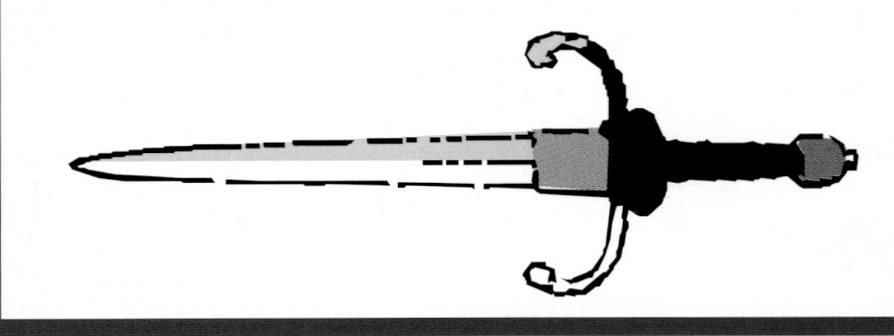

20

Duncan's goodness is contrasted with the 'deep damnation' of the act of murder. This is a direct comparison of the spiritual state of the two men, Duncan and Macbeth, his killer. Macbeth realises that he would be damned for eternity for such a sinful act.

SHAKESPEARE'S LANGUAGE – *MACBETH*

The witches have predicted that Macbeth will be king. He and his wife have planned to murder King Duncan. In this soliloquy, Macbeth is having second thoughts.

LANGUAGE DEVICES

- Alliteration is used for emphasis in this speech – 'trumpet-tongued', 'deep damnation', 'naked newborn babe'.
- Throughout this soliloquy, Macbeth uses euphemisms for the murder of Duncan, e.g. 'bear the knife', 'his taking-off', 'horrid deed'. This shows that Macbeth is reluctant to think about the brutality of the act of murder. He is trying to avoid the reality of the situation and cannot face up to the evil nature of the plan that he and his wife have made.
- At the end of this soliloquy, Macbeth has convinced himself not to go ahead with the murder. This part of the soliloquy is in three sections: the reasons why the murder is wrong (lines 12–18); Macbeth's fear of discovery and eternal damnation (lines 18–25) and his want of a 'good' reason to commit the crime (lines 25–28).

21–25

He uses images of innocence and purity – the newborn baby and the cherubin (the highest order of angels) – as the messengers of Duncan's death. They are described as riding the winds (sightless couriers) like horses. Just as a cold wind brings tears to your eyes this news will bring tears to everybody's eyes. He imagines that the winds will be drowned with tears. This emphasises the scale of public mourning for the death of such a king.

25–28

In comparison to all the reasons not to kill Duncan, his only reason to carry out the murder is his ambition. He compares his ambition to a horse that tries to jump too high and falls on the other side of the fence. Macbeth thinks that if he gives in to ambition, he will fail in the end.

Examiner's Top Tip

Remember that religion and the consequences of sin were very important in Shakespeare's time. The power of the language in this soliloquy comes from the religious references.

SHAKESPEARE – REVISION TECHNIQUES AND TASKS

The following ideas will help you to organise your thoughts about the play you have studied. Once you have completed these tasks, the best way to revise is to answer practice questions. You will find some example questions in the test section.

Make a time line of important events in the play. Leave space to make notes about connections between the scenes. For example:

TWELFTH NIGHT

CONNECTIONS	EVENTS
	– Orsino is in love with Olivia
*Viola's disguise leads to unhappiness.	– Viola is shipwrecked, she fears her brother, Sebastian, is dead. She plans to disguise herself as a man and serve Orsino*
She loves Orsino; he loves Olivia; she loves Cesario/Viola	– Viola /Cesario is trusted with all Orsino's secrets and sent to woo Olivia. Viola is in love with Orsino.*
	– Sebastian is rescued by Antonio
	– Olivia reveals her love for Cesario*

Make spider diagrams for each of the main characters to trace plot involvement, relationships and personality. For example:

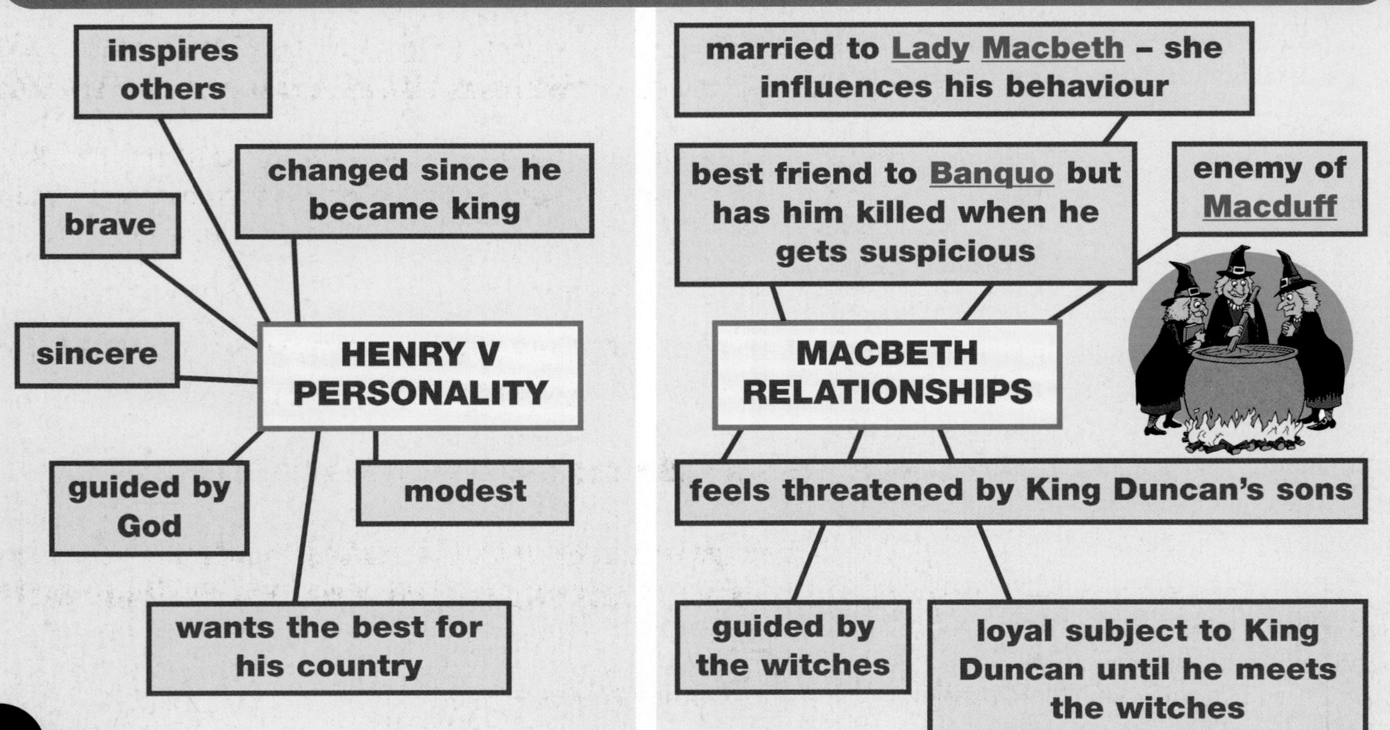

KEY THEMES

Pick out the key themes in your scene and find quotations that link to this theme in other scenes. If you have your own copy of the play, mark the quotations in your text, using a different colour for each theme. If you don't have your own copy then write out the quotations and colour-code them.

LANGUAGE

Make a close study of the language used by the main characters in your scene. Think about:

- **how it helps to create an atmosphere**
- **how it helps to show the development of relationships**
- **what it shows us about the personality or intentions of those characters.**

ACTION IN THE REST OF THE PLAY

Make a list or table to show:

- how the action in your scene is affected by preceding scenes
- how the action in your scene affects the rest of the play.

Practice questions

Practice questions from the three possible question groups: empathy, literary criticism and staging. You will find some example questions on the following pages.

HENRY V

King:
Now are we well resolv'd, and by God's help
And yours, the noble sinews of our power,
France being ours, we'll bend it to our awe,
Or break it all to pieces. Or there we'll sit,
Ruling in large and ample empery
O'er France and all her almost kingly dukedoms,
Or lay these bones in an unworthy urn
Tombless, with no remembrance over them.
Either our history shall with full mouth
Speak freely of our acts, or else our grave
Like Turkish mute shall have a tongueless mouth,
Not worshipp'd with a waxen epitaph.

We are no tyrant, but a Christian king,
Unto whose grace our passion is as subject
As are our wretches fettered in our prisons.
Therefore with frank and with uncurbed plainness
Tell us the Dauphin's mind.

Henry V **(Act 1, Scene 2, lines 222–233 and 241–245)**

MACBETH

Macbeth:
That will never be:
Who can impress the forest, bid the tree
Unfix his earth-bound root? Sweet bodements! Good!
Rebellion's head, rise never till the wood
Of Birnam rise, and our high-plac'd Macbeth
Shall live the lease of nature, pay his breath
To time and mortal custom. Yet my heart
Throbs to know one thing: tell me – if your art
Can tell so much – shall Banquo's issue ever
Reign in this kingdom?

(aside) Time, thou anticipat'st my dread exploits;
The flighty purpose never is o'ertook
Unless the deed go with it; from this moment
The very firstlings of my heart shall be
The firstlings of my hand. And even now,
To crown my thoughts with acts, be it thought and done:
The castle of Macduff I will surprise;
Seize upon Fife; give to the edge of the sword
His wife, his babes, and all unfortunate souls
That trace him in his line. No boasting like a fool;
This deed I'll do before this purpose cool:

Macbeth **(Act 4, Scene 1, lines 94–103 and 144–154)**

SHAKESPEARE LANGUAGE STUDY – *MACBETH, TWELFTH NIGHT* AND *HENRY V*

Make a close study of the language in the extract from your play. Important words, phrases and language devices have been identified to help you.

TWELFTH NIGHT

Examiner's Top Tip
Follow the example on the previous page. Think carefully about why particular words and phrases have been used.

Orsino:
If music be the food of love, play on;
Give me excess of it, that surfeiting,
The appetite may sicken and so die.
That strain again, it had a dying fall;
O it came o'er my ear like the sweet sound
That breathes upon a bank of violets,
Stealing and giving odour. Enough; no more.
'Tis not so sweet now as it was before.
O spirit of love, how quick and fresh art thou,
That, notwithstanding thy capacity,
Receiveth as the sea. Nought enters there,
Of what validity and pitch soe'er,
But falls into abatement and low price
Even in a minute. So full of shapes is fancy,
That it alone is high fantastical.

Curio: **Will you go hunt, my lord?**
Orsino: **What, Curio?**

Curio: **The hart.**
Orsino: **Why so I do, the noblest that I have.**
O when mine eyes did see Olivia first,
Methought she purged the air of pestilence;
That instant was I turned into a hart,
And my desires like fell and cruel hounds
E'er since pursue me.

***Twelfth Night* (Act 1, Scene 1, lines 1–23)**

SHAKESPEARE TEST

- Always use the bullet points with the question to help plan your answer. The mark scheme is based on these bullet points.
- Remember you must support your opinions with relevant quotations and textual evidence.
- These mock exam questions are very general so that they can be applied to any scene. Try to answer these questions for your specified scene.

EMPATHY

1. Imagine you are the central character in the scene. Write about how you feel about the events you have been involved in and what you plan to do next.

STAGING

2. You are the director of the play. Write detailed instructions for how each of the main characters should be played in this scene
   Think about:

- how they should move
- how they should behave
- how they should speak
- what their relationships should be with other characters.

LITERARY CRITICISM

3. Choose the most appropriate question for your scene from the list below. With all questions you should consider the following:

- the behaviour of the characters
- use of language
- what has happened before the scene and what happens next.

4. How is the atmosphere created or changed in this scene?
   Think about:

- how the characters would behave
- what the main characters would be thinking – are they hiding anything?
- what has just happened or is about to happen.

5. Comment on the behaviour of the main character in this scene.
   Think about:

Reading Media Texts – Quick Questions

1. There is a balance of fact and opinions. Facts: information about the service, makes it seem reliable: 'operates 24-hours a day'. Opinion: reassuring, makes the service providers seem like friends: 'we'll always be there for you'.
2. Front cover: woman looking out of her window, isolated and worried; call centre operator, friendly and helpful. The two pictures show that there is a solution to the problem of loneliness. Inside the leaflet: men and women wearing the SeniorLink pendants, happy and relaxed; call button is small and doesn't get in the way.

3 Personal pronouns: makes the leaflet personalised, a direct invitation to the reader to find out more: 'You need never feel...', 'We believe that you should always feel safe.' This would appeal to older people who feel lonely or live away from their family.

4 Pictures: as above. Bullet points: easy to read. Bold type: highlights important information. Columns and short paragraphs: quick and easy to read. Slogan: direct message, reassuring.

Spelling: Plurals – Quick Questions

benches	foxes	churches	pupils	lights	wishes	washes
boys	fries	flies	monkeys	plays	babies	ladies
radios	volcanoes	shampoos	goes			
wolves	knives	lives	loaves	roofs		
men	women	geese	feet			

Spelling: Prefixes and Suffixes – Quick Questions

disappoint	disappointment	disappointed	disappointing	appointment
appointed	appointing			
unfortunate	unfortunately	fortunately		
preview	previewed	previewing	viewed	viewing
uneventful	uneventfully	eventful	eventfully	
misunderstand	misunderstanding	understanding	understandingly	

Punctuation Marks – Quick Questions

1. 'Shut up!' shouted James. 'You don't know what you're talking about.'
2. 'I want to go home now mum,' whispered the bored child.
3. 'Have you seen my sister?' asked Simon.
   'No, I haven't seen her since yesterday,' said Julie.
4. I saw James, the boy who broke his leg, on the BBC news last night.
5. When the bell rang, the teacher dismissed the class.
6. My sister, who's a nurse, helped to bandage my leg.

Apostrophes – Quick Questions

don't	they'll	haven't	I'm	wouldn't

the man's strength	the girl's bags (singular)	the girls' bags (plural)
yesterday's meeting	Laura's ambition	

INDEX